Pearson

Year
6

Grammar and Punctuation
Activity Workbook

Author:
Hannah
Hirst-Dunton

Published by Pearson Education Limited, 80 Strand, London, WC2R 0RL.
www.pearsonschools.co.uk

Text © Pearson Education Limited 2022
Edited by Florence Production Ltd
Designed by Pearson Education Limited 2022
Typeset by Florence Production Ltd
Produced by Florence Production Ltd and Sarah Loader
Original illustrations © Pearson Education Limited 2022
Cover design by Pearson Education Limited 2022

The right of Hannah Hirst-Dunton to be identified as author of this work has been asserted by her in
accordance with the Copyright, Designs and Patents Act 1988.

First published 2022

25 24 23 22
10 9 8 7 6 5 4 3 2 1

British Library Cataloguing in Publication Data
A catalogue record for this book is available from the British Library

ISBN 978 1 292 42502 3

Printed in Slovakia by Neografia

Acknowledgements
Front Cover: Neonic Flower/Shutterstock, Anna Frajtova/Shutterstock, Mascha Tace/Shutterstock
Design: © Pearson Education Limited, 2021

The author and publisher would like to thank the following individuals and organisations for permission
to reproduce photographs:

(Key: b-bottom; c-centre; l-left; r-right; t-top)

Shutterstock: Olga Utchenko iv, 12, 18, 23, 33, 45, 70, 78; Spreadthedesign iv, 12, 18, 23, 33, 45, 70, 78;
Tegah Mujiono iv, 12, 18, 23, 33, 45, 70, 78

All other images © Pearson Education Limited

Notes from the publisher
Pearson has robust editorial processes, including answer and fact checks, to ensure the accuracy of the
content in this publication, and every effort is made to ensure this publication is free of errors. We are,
however, only human, and occasionally errors do occur. Pearson is not liable for any misunderstandings
that arise as a result of errors in this publication, but it is our priority to ensure that the content is
accurate. If you spot an error, please do contact us at resourcescorrections@pearson.com so we can
make sure it is corrected.

Contents

About this book

This book will help your child to improve their basic literacy skills, fill gaps in learning and increase confidence in a fun and engaging way. It offers a simple, approachable way for you to guide your child through the grammar and punctuation requirements of the National Curriculum.

Your child's mastery of grammar will allow them to express themselves clearly and meet expectations within the whole English curriculum, and beyond!

Grammar and punctuation made clear

Grammar guide

From **whom** did you get a letter?   **Who** did you get a letter **from**?

- The relative pronoun '**whom**' is usually used in only formal language.
- It is used rather than '**who**' as the object in a sentence.
- In formal language, a **preposition** should never be placed at the end of a sentence. It comes before the object of the sentence instead.

Rewrite each sentence using vocabulary that is more formal.

1 Sorry for showing up late.

_I apologise for_____

2 Who shall I hand over the present to?

_____

- This activity book is split into bite-sized, manageable topics that are clearly named.

- Each topic is broken down into a number of sessions that develop particular skills and understanding.

- Every session includes grammar or punctuation guides, which give 'at a glance' guidance.

- Then three activities introduce, practise and reinforce the skill focus.

- Completing all three activities in one sitting will help your child get to grips with the concept.

- There are checkpoints for your child to fill in at the end of each topic. This gives you the chance to see where further support is needed.

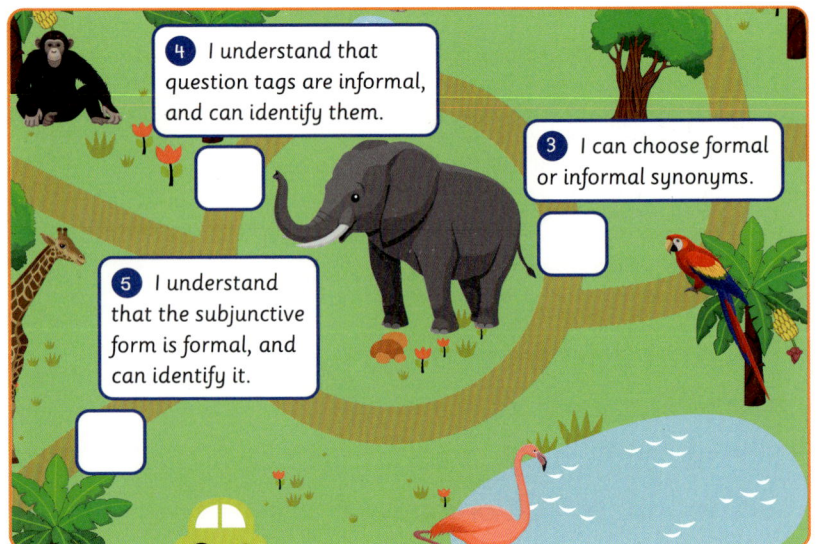

4 I understand that question tags are informal, and can identify them.

3 I can choose formal or informal synonyms.

5 I understand that the subjunctive form is formal, and can identify it.

How to use this book

- Short sessions work best. Try setting aside half an hour for your child to explore the three activities.

- Try to complete the topics in the given order, as many of them form key foundations for the ones that follow them.

- Your child will ideally work through topics independently, but it's worth being there for when support is needed.

Building from ...

These topics follow on directly from Year 5 to Year 6:

Year 5 topic	Year 6 topic
Exploring adverbials	Adjectives, adverbials and prepositions
Verb forms	Further verb forms
Relative clauses	Formal and informal registers
Punctuation	Punctuation

- If your child seems bored or is struggling, suggest they take a break. It might be that they understand the ideas already, or just need time to take something in. They could work on a creative task, such as colouring or following patterns. Try the Pearson Handwriting Activity Workbooks: they contain lots of fun activities, and will also help your child to practise pencil control.

- At the end of a topic, explore the checkpoints with your child and make sure you're happy with what they've understood.

Building towards ...

As children progress into Year 7, grammar and punctuation remain highly valuable.

The National Curriculum for children in Years 7–9 states they should use their understanding by:

- extending and applying the grammatical knowledge [...] to analyse more challenging texts
- studying the effectiveness and impact of the grammatical features of the texts they read
- knowing and understanding the differences between [...] formal and informal registers, and between Standard English and other varieties of English
- using Standard English confidently in their own writing and speech
- discussing reading, writing and spoken language with precise and confident use of linguistic and literary terminology.

Getting started

- Make your child's learning space interesting and fun, in a favourite place to sit or with a favourite toy beside them.
- Encourage your child to step away from any technology or energetic games a little while beforehand, and to take some deep breaths to help them focus.
- Make sure they're sitting comfortably at a table and holding their pencil properly.
- Try to sit with your child to start, even if you're occupied with your own task.

A helping hand

Remind your child to ask for help when they need it. In some topics, you may find they need a little extra guidance. Follow the tips below to support them.

The passive voice (pages 19–23)

Both 'Activity 3' tasks quickly test children's familiarity with all the verb forms they have learned. If your child lacks confidence, look back at the revision in the Year 5 Activity Book.

> **Activity 3**
>
> Draw lines to match each sentence to its tense and form.
>
> | | |
> |---|---|
> | The cake was eaten by Tina. | simple past, active voice |
> | We were running home. | simple past, passive voice |
> | The ball has been kicked by Marco. | past progressive, active voic |
> | I was cold. | present perfect, passive voic |

> Explain the differences between each pair of words.
>
> ❶ quickly — in a hurry
>
> One means they were just fast and the other means they were doi
> things more quickly than usual because they didn't have much time.
>
> ❷ dislike — hate
> _____

Synonyms and antonyms: Choosing synonyms carefully (pages 26–28)

Activity 2 challenges children to note subtle differences between near-synonyms. Your child may have trouble putting their ideas into words: it may help for them to discuss rather than to write their answers.

> **Activity 3**
>
> Write the meaning of each formal word.
>
> ❶ subsequently _____
> ❷ fabricate _____
> ❸ amicable _____

Formal and informal registers (pages 34–45)

During this topic, children are challenged to give informal alternatives to formal terms. If they struggle with any of the terms' meanings, encourage them to use a dictionary.

Punctuation: How can hyphens help with clarity? (pages 46–47) and
Using hyphens for clarity (pages 48–49)

Your child may find it both fun and helpful to say the sentences aloud and discuss them. Suggest that they use these given sentences as models for writing their own.

> Draw lines to show the meaning of each word.
>
> | | |
> |---|---|
> | re-sign | sent again |
> | resign | sign again |
> | re-sent | quit |
> | resent | dislike |

Tricky concepts

Formal language

Children may believe that formal language is 'fancy' language. Encourage them to think of it as just precise and polite instead.

Bullet points

Many people are inconsistent when writing bullet points. Ensure that your child uses the same format for all points in one list: for example, all complete sentences or all past-tense verbs. You could ask them to check by writing the content as a list sentence that isn't bulleted.

Technical terms

Even when children know and understand the structures of grammar, terminology can make things seem difficult. Help your child to use the Glossary, which makes the terms clearer.

Progress check

- Once your child has worked on some activities, judge how confident they are with carrying on alone. If they're keen for independence, they're probably on the right track.
- Encourage your child to talk to you about what they are learning. Getting an explanation in their own words will show you how much they've understood.

Extension activities

- Challenge your child to rearrange conjunctions, end punctuation, colons, semicolons and dashes in passages from reading materials.
- Expand your child's understanding of synonyms and antonyms by providing a thesaurus. This will give them a chance to explore more examples and to practise their research skills.
- Encourage your child to apply their understanding of both cohesive devices and non-fiction features by writing engaging and eye-catching adverts.

Putting grammar and punctuation skills to use

Help your child to understand that their new grammar and punctuation skills are in use everywhere. Encourage them to find examples around them, including in their reading materials.

- Prompt your child to think imaginatively about different text types. Posters and magazines contain some fun features they could use themselves.
- Show your child examples of formal language in context by sharing official letters with them.

1: Exploring adjectives

Activity 1

> ### Grammar guide
>
> I drew a **big, bright picture** of a **leafy green tree**.
> I knew I'd done a **good drawing**: it was certainly the **most colourful picture**.
>
> - **Adjectives** add information about **nouns**.
> - Multiple adjectives are usually separated by **commas**, like items in a list.
> - You do not need to add a comma if one of the adjectives is 'absolute'. An absolute adjective is one that cannot take the adverb 'very'.
> - An **adjectival phrase** is a group of words that forms one piece of added information.
> - Adjectival phrases include adverbs that add information to the head adjective.

1 Underline the adjectives and adjectival phrases.

    a Her <u>youngest</u> sister went to a different school.

    b Jamal knew he should be making a much bigger effort to help out.

2 Add adjectives or adjectival phrases to expand the noun phrases.

    a Last night, I ate some _____ food.

    b The _____ book was our favourite.

Activity 2

Grammar guide

Kerri's drawing was **better** and **more interesting** than mine.
Rani's was the **best** and **most interesting** drawing in the class.

- **Comparative adjectives** compare the qualities of two or more nouns.
- **Superlative adjectives** compare the qualities of three or more nouns.
  They show that the quality being described is the most extreme.

1 Rewrite the following sentences, changing the adjectives to comparative adjectives.

I read a good book last week. It had a surprise twist at the end.

I read a better book last week.

_____

2 Rewrite the following sentences, changing the adjectives to superlative adjectives.

That's a funny poem. It has amusing illustrations.

_____

_____

Activity 3

Look back at Activity 1, Question 1. Label each sentence there as comparative or superlative to show what kind of adjective it contains.

2: Exploring prepositions

Activity 1

Grammar guide

> Arthit occupies **the desk by the window**.
> Arthit occupies **the desk** <u>that is **by the window**</u>.

- A **prepositional phrase** can be used to expand a **noun phrase**.
- It can link connected ideas about the noun's quality, place, time or cause.
- It could be part of a <u>relative clause</u>.

Identify the expanded noun phrase in each sentence and underline it once. Underline each prepositional phrase twice.

1. <u>The shed <u>at the end of the garden</u></u> was falling apart.
2. The moon's reflection on the lake was beautiful.
3. I noticed the grey clouds above us were disappearing.

Activity 2

Grammar guide

> <u>In my opinion</u>, Arthit has the best desk <u>in the room</u>.

- <u>Prepositional phrases</u> can be **adverbials** rather than **parts of noun phrases** if they add information about something other than just a noun, pronoun or noun phrase.
- It is important to understand when they are being used correctly as part of a noun phrase.
- If a prepositional phrase could be moved around in its sentence, it is probably an adverbial.

1 Underline the prepositions in the following sentences. Tick the sentences that use prepositional phrases in noun phrases.

a The stain on the carpet wouldn't come out. ◯

b Woodland creatures often hibernate over the winter. ◯

c Our route through the city was blocked. ◯

d The show during half time was amazing. ◯

e The clock chimed at midnight. ◯

2 Add a prepositional phrase to each sentence to expand the underlined noun phrase. Take care not to add it as an adverbial.

a I ran quickly through <u>the tunnel</u>.

<u>I ran quickly through the tunnel under the railway tracks.</u>

b The picture fell onto <u>the table</u>.

_____

c <u>The show</u> was a hit.

_____

Activity 3

Write a sentence that uses the prepositional phrase below as part of a noun phrase.

on the shelf

_____

_____

_____

3: Exploring relative clauses

Activity 1

Grammar guide

I wave at **the girl** <u>who is standing by the door</u>.

- A **relative pronoun** connects a noun or **noun phrase** to information related to it.
- The pronoun and the related information make up a <u>relative clause</u>.
- The relative pronouns are 'who', 'whose', 'whom', 'that', 'which', 'when' and 'where'.
  - 'Who', 'whose' and 'whom' relate to people.
  - 'Which' and 'that' refer to things or ideas.
  - 'When' refers to a time.
  - 'Where' refers to a place.

Underline each relative clause. Circle each relative pronoun. Write what each relative pronoun represents: a person, thing, time or place.

1 Ruby longed for the day when she could return home. _____

2 Rob's ideal pet would be a cat that didn't make him sneeze. _____

3 The mayor, to whom I wrote last week, did not respond. _____

4 This is the train's last stop, where we have to catch a bus. _____

Activity 2

Grammar guide

I need <u>a pen</u> **that is red**. This is my pen, **which is red**.

- A **definitive relative clause** adds information that is vital to meaning.
- An **incidental relative clause** adds information that is not vital.
- 'That' begins only definitive clauses. 'Which' begins only incidental clauses.
- Other relative pronouns can begin both definitive and incidental relative clauses.
- A definitive relative clause becomes a part of the <u>noun phrase</u>, rather than extra detail.

1 Select one of the relative pronouns below to complete each noun phrase. Use each only once.

whom   whose   who

a This is the woman _____ gave me such good advice.

b The boy _____ wallet was lost searched frantically.

c The teacher _____ you are seeking is no longer here.

2 Add a definite relative clause to complete the noun phrase in each of the following sentences.

a That was the moment _____

_____

b This is the beach _____

_____

Activity 3

1 Add 'which' and 'that' in the correct positions.

I broke the cup _____ I was washing,

_____ wasn't good.

2 Write the whole of the noun phrase that is now in the sentence above.

_____

4: Combining information in noun phrases

Activity 1

Grammar guide

I've lost a **new** **phone** **with a red case** **that is scratched**.

- A <u>noun phrase</u> can be expanded using **adjectives**, **prepositional phrases** and **definitive relative clauses**.
- A relative clause could add information straight to the **lead noun** or a noun within the prepositional phrase. They are all in one noun phrase that describes the lead noun.

Expand each simple noun phrase using any combination of the adjectives, prepositional phrases and relative clauses below.

Adjectives	Prepositional phrases	Relative clauses
biggest	in the shop	that we liked
lovelier	with all those stars	where we met
warm	from the holiday	that we found

1 those hats

 those warm hats in the shop that we found

2 the place

_____

3 that trip

_____

Activity 2

> I've lost a bag. The bag is big. The bag has straps. You gave me the bag as a gift.
>
> I've lost the **big** bag **with straps** **that you gave me as a gift**.

- Lots of information can be put together into one noun phrase.
- The information could be added in any of the ways that a noun phrase can be expanded: as an **adjective**, as a **prepositional phrase** or as a **relative clause**.

Combine all of the information in each set of sentences into one noun phrase. Think carefully about the relative pronouns you choose.

1 That's the lady. The lady is old. The lady has purple hair. The lady smiles kindly.

That's the old lady with purple hair who smiles kindly.

2 I went back to the forest. The forest was beautiful. The forest is on the hill. We once had a picnic in the forest.

I went back to _____

_____

3 I saw a bird. The bird was enormous. The bird had orange spots. The bird was singing.

I saw _____

_____

4 Philly is that boy. Philly is young. Philly is in the armchair. Philly is waving.

Philly is _____

_____

5 That was the day. The day was glorious. The day was during the summer. We met on the day.

That was _____

_____

Activity 3

Look at the sentences. Change each one into four sentences that give the information. (This exercise is the reverse of the one in Activity 2.)

1 She had a fluffy cat with grey ears that purred loudly.

<u>She had a cat. The cat was fluffy. The cat had grey ears.</u>

<u>The cat purred loudly.</u>

2 We're going to the new cinema in town where there are sofas.

_____

_____

3 He looked for the kind stranger on the train who had helped him.

_____

_____

What do I Know?

1 I can identify adjectives and adjectival phrases.

2 I can use comparative and superlative adjectives.

3 I can identify prepositional phrases in expanded noun phrases.

5 I understand how different relative pronouns can be used.

4 I can write prepositional phrases that are parts of noun phrases.

6 I can use definitive and incidental relative clauses in writing.

7 I can use adjectives, prepositional phrases and relative clauses to put information together in noun phrases.

1: Revising adverbials

Activity 1

Grammar guide

- If a piece of writing has cohesion, different parts of it are linked together to become effective as a whole.
- **Fronted adverbials** can be used to create cohesion between paragraphs.
- They can signal a text's structure clearly for the reader.

> I would argue that a shorter school day would mean pupils are well rested.
>
> Consequently, they would be able to concentrate better. They could focus harder during the hours they were studying.
>
> In contrast, the hours they now spend working are exhausting. They additionally prevent relaxation so pupils also resent their studies.
>
> In summary, I believe everyone would benefit.

Comment on the effects the adverbials create in the passage above.

Consequently: The next point is a result of the one before it.

_____

_____

_____

_____

Activity 2

> Add fronted adverbials you feel would help to structure this passage of short paragraphs.

Is Exploring Space Really Important?

<u>Currently</u>, governments around the world spend huge amounts of money on exploring space. Whether or not they should do this is often debated.

_____, the UK government said it would spend nearly £2 billion on space programmes between 2019 and 2024. The budget of NASA (the US government's space agency) was $22.6 billion for 2020 alone.

_____, there are many problems on Earth that could be helped by this money. It can be argued that that environmental problems deserve it more. Issues like climate change, the destruction of rainforests and illegal hunting need a lot of resources if they are ever going to be stopped.

_____, space exploration has been responsible for many scientific breakthroughs that benefit us. These include artificial limbs, firefighting equipment, wireless headphones and the tiny cameras that are now in phones. They also include solar panels, which help to solve some of the world's environmental problems.

_____, it is a complicated subject. We can see the problems on Earth, and they are affecting us now. We don't know what problems could be solved in the future by research into space travel.

Activity 3

> Look again at the passages in Activities 1 and 2. Write down any adverbials you could use to create different links between the short paragraphs.

_____

_____

_____

2: What are cohesive devices?

Activity 1

Grammar guide

> **We can help you to p**lan. **We can help you to p**repare.
> **We can help you to p**ass those tests.
> The **fun** has just be**gun** at Glad**stone** Park!
> <u>So, why were the Vikings so successful?</u>
> <u>They were excellent sailors and ruthless fighters.</u>

- There are lots of ways to create cohesion.
- Fronted adverbials are one example of cohesive devices. Pronouns are another, because they can refer back to earlier subjects and objects.
- There are many other devices writers and speakers use to create cohesion within or between sentences. They are often designed to sound engaging. They include:
    - repeating ideas, **phrases**, words or **sounds**
    - creating **rhymes** or **near-rhymes**
    - <u>asking</u> and then <u>answering</u> questions.
- Devices like these are particularly good at creating powerful cohesion in short pieces of writing like adverts.

Describe the cohesive device or devices in each example.

1 We've promised a lot during this presentation, but can we deliver? I guarantee it.

The sentences ask and answer a question. They also repeat 'p' in 'promised' and 'presentation'.

2 The secret of success is to practise, practise and practise some more.

_____

_____

3 What will you read next? Will you choose the satisfaction of action? Is it time for crime? How about some frantic romantic tales?

_____

_____

Activity 2

1 Write a question and answer to get a reader interested in a book about the rainforest.

_____

_____

2 Use repetition of a sound to create a motto for your school or your family.

_____

_____

3 Use repetition of a word to create some persuasive instructions for being helpful around the house.

_____

_____

4 Use at least one rhyme to create a short advertising slogan for a company that sells school clothes. You could use some of the rhyming words below, or any words of your own.

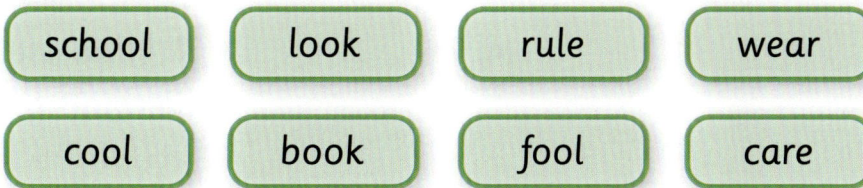

| school | look | rule | wear |
| cool | book | fool | care |

_____

_____

Activity 3

Write a short paragraph designed to persuade someone you would be a good leader. Use at least two different cohesive devices.

_____

_____

_____

_____

_____

_____

What do I Know?

1. I understand how fronted adverbials can create cohesion between paragraphs.

2. I can use fronted adverbials to create effective links between paragraphs.

3. I understand how repetition, rhyme and questions can create cohesion within or between sentences.

4. I can use different cohesive devices to create effective writing.

1: What is the passive voice?

Activity 1

Grammar guide ··

> **My friend carried my bag**.

- Sentences are usually written in the 'active' voice.
- The **subject** of a sentence is the noun, noun phrase or pronoun that is the focus of that sentence. In an 'active' sentence, it names the thing or person performing the action named by the **verb**.
- The **object** of a sentence is usually a noun, noun phrase or pronoun that is involved with an action but does not perform it, and it comes just after the **verb**. In an 'active' sentence, it names the thing or person that the **verb** is 'done to' or 'done with'.
- There can be more than one subject and more than one object in a sentence.

> Circle the subjects and underline the objects.

1. She handed over the magazine.
2. Georgie often ate apples.
3. Someone should please sharpen the pencils.
4. Kim and his mum picked fruit and vegetables.

Activity 2

Grammar guide

My bag **was** carried by **my friend**. My diary was discovered.

- Sentences in the 'passive' voice describe an **action** that is being done to the **subject**, rather than something that the subject is doing.
- The action could be done by the **object**, or **by something or someone unknown**.
- The passive form uses the **auxiliary verb 'to be'** and a **past participle**.

Circle the subjects and underline any objects. Then label each sentence as active or passive

1. That play was seen by all of us. _____

2. Jayne and Li are both confused by modern art. _____

3. You are never satisfied. _____

4. Franco's letter has been returned. _____

5. Brad is a fan of old records. _____

Activity 3

Draw lines to match each sentence to its tense and form.

The cake was eaten by Tina.	simple past, active voice
We were running home.	simple past, passive voice
The ball has been kicked by Marco.	past progressive, active voice
I was cold.	present perfect, passive voice

2: Using the passive voice

Activity 1

Grammar guide

- Sentences in the passive voice describe an action that is being done to the subject, rather than something that the subject is doing.
- The passive form uses the auxiliary verb 'to be' and a past participle.

Rewrite the sentences using the passive voice.

1 Asha often helps Ma.

 Ma is often helped by Asha.

2 We have painted the chest of drawers.

_____

3 That heron is catching fish.

_____

Activity 2

Grammar guide

The vase was broken by **the twins**. **It was shattered.**

- The passive voice can focus a sentence on **the action**.
- **The person or thing doing the action** could be left out.

> Create an effective story from the sentences below.
>
> For each pair of sentences, choose and underline either the one using the active voice or the one using the passive voice. In the passive sentences, you can choose to keep or miss out the information in brackets. Underline it if you choose to keep it.

- Two days ago, the Vaunting family discovered something mysterious.
  <u>Two days ago, a mysterious event was discovered</u> (by the Vaunting family).
- Someone had stolen a priceless emerald necklace.
  A priceless emerald necklace had been stolen (by someone).
- The Vaunting family called me, Private Detective Semaphore.
  I, Private Detective Semaphore, was called (by the Vaunting family).
- I searched the grounds of their home, but I found no clues.
  The grounds of their home were searched (by me), but no clues were found (by me).
- Lady Vaunting has asked me to carry out interviews.
  I have been asked to carry out interviews (by Lady Vaunting).
- However, until now, I have suspected nobody.
  However, until now, nobody has been suspected (by me).

Activity 3

> Rewrite the sentence below in each different tense and form.

I search the house.

1 simple past tense, passive voice

_____

2 past-perfect tense, passive voice

_____

3 present-progressive tense, passive voice

_____

What do I Know?

1 I understand and can identify passive sentences.

2 I can identify the subjects and objects in passive sentences.

3 I can identify the subject and objects in passive sentences.

4 I can form sentences in the passive voice, in different tenses.

5 I can select where the passive voice is most effective.

1: What are synonyms?

Activity 1

Grammar guide

I **put** the kettle on the stove. I **placed** the kettle on the stove.

- **Synonyms** are words or phrases that have the same or very similar meanings.
- They could be swapped for each other in a sentence without changing the sentence's meaning.

Draw lines to match each word or phrase to its nearest synonym.

come	buy
sprint	display
show	hold
false	arrive
get	run
grip	fake

Activity 2

Swap the underlined word in each sentence with its nearest synonym from the words below.

| smash | used up | fresh | huge | support |

1 The goalkeeper made a <u>big</u> mistake.

   <u>The goalkeeper made a huge mistake.</u>

2 Geraint <u>spent</u> all his money by renting movies.

   _____

3 That's his <u>new</u> bike.

   _____

4 Did you <u>break</u> your brother's model?

   _____

5 Leah asked me for <u>help</u> at school.

   _____

Activity 3

Look again at your answers to Activity 2. Did all the synonym pairs mean exactly the same thing as each other? Which one or ones do you think changed most in meaning? Why is that?

_____

_____

2: Choosing synonyms carefully

Activity 1

cover: bedsheet, jacket, lid, shelter; bury, conceal, protect, study

- There can be many synonyms for some words, especially if the word has different meanings or can be different types of word (such as a noun or a verb).
- It's import to think about the context of the synonym you choose: the situation in which it's used.

Tick a box to show which synonym would be the best in each sentence.

1 The family next door <u>has</u> a silver car.

☐ holds   ☐ owns

2 Felicia made <u>plans</u> for the weekend.

☐ maps   ☐ arrangements

3 Year 6 put on a <u>show</u> for the parents.

☐ performance   ☐ reveal

4 Something about the silence was really <u>odd</u>.

☐ unpaired   ☐ strange

Activity 2

Grammar guide

My quiz answers were incorrect. It was wrong of me to rely on guesswork.
My quiz answers were correct. It was right of me to study hard.

- Sometimes, the differences between synonyms' meanings are small.
  They are still important.
- For example, the words 'wrong' and 'right' may be treated as synonyms
  for 'incorrect' and 'correct'. However, 'incorrect' and 'correct' describe
  just accuracy. 'Wrong' and 'right' can suggest something moral, like
  'good' and 'bad'.

Explain the differences between each pair of words.

1   quickly   in a hurry

   One means they were just fast and the other means they were doing

   things more quickly than usual because they didn't have much time.

2   dislike   hate

_____

_____

3   wonder   consider

_____

_____

4   think   believe

_____

_____

Activity 3

Replace the underlined words in these sentences with synonyms. You could use words or phrases.

On Thursday, Jakub <u>went</u> into town to buy a <u>present</u> for his sister. He <u>looked</u> for ages for something she'd <u>like</u>. Finally, he <u>found</u> something perfect.

_____

_____

_____

_____

3: What are antonyms?

Activity 1

Grammar guide

He **gave** the gift. She **kept** the gift.

- **Antonyms** are words or phrases that have opposite or very different meanings.
- Swapping them can reverse the meaning of a sentence.
- Some straightforward antonyms can be formed by simply adding 'un–'.

Draw lines to match each word or phrase to its antonym.

love	bad
beautiful	unfriendly
friendly	leave
wide	hate
arrive	narrow
good	ugly

Activity 2

Swap the underlined word in each sentence with its nearest synonym from the words below.

worst   disappointed   unhelpful   always   impossible

1. Sota was usually <u>helpful</u> around the house.

   <u>Sota was usually unhelpful around the house.</u>

2. It <u>never</u> rains on her birthday.

   _____

3. That's the <u>best</u> idea I've heard in ages!

   _____

4. It was <u>certain</u> that they'd see him again.

   _____

5. I'm so <u>pleased</u> you could get here!

   _____

Activity 3

Look again at your answers to Activity 2. Did all the words have precise antonyms that meant exactly the opposite? Which one or ones didn't?

_____

_____

_____

4: Choosing effective antonyms

Activity 1

| I dislike it. I hate it. I detest it. | | I like it. I love it. I adore it. |

- There are usually lots of options that could be considered a word's antonym. The options are synonyms of each other.
- Thinking about degrees of meaning as well as context can be helpful, but this is not the only way to choose an effective antonym.

Looking at the degrees of meaning, tick a box to show which antonym more directly pairs with each underlined word.

1   **a**   The trip was <u>good</u>.   ✓ bad   ☐ terrible

     b   The trip was <u>wonderful</u>.   ☐ bad   ✓ terrible

2   **a**   It was a <u>warm</u> day.   ☐ cold   ☐ cool

     b   It was a <u>hot</u> day.   ☐ cold   ☐ cool

3   **a**   Sylvia looked <u>happy</u>.   ☐ devastated   ☐ sad

     b   Sylvia look <u>overjoyed</u>.   ☐ devastated   ☐ sad

4   **a**   The book's message was <u>confusing</u>.   ☐ clear   ☐ obvious

     b   The book's message was <u>baffling</u>.   ☐ clear   ☐ obvious

Activity 2

Write three antonyms for each underlined word. Select the one you think is the most effective, and rewrite the sentence using it.

1 That was an <u>interesting</u> film.

Antonyms: _____boring_____ _____ _____

_____

2 He felt so <u>frightened</u> in the dark.

Antonyms: _____ _____ _____

_____

3 The blanket felt warm and <u>soft</u>.

Antonyms: _____ _____ _____

_____

Activity 3

Grammar guide

The car was **green**.   The car was **red**.

- Usually, only very extreme or clear things can have direct opposites.
- **Some words have very different meanings**, but aren't antonyms.

It is hard to find opposites of the underlined words below. Note down alternative words that would make the sentences' meanings as different as possible.

1 The morning was cold and <u>misty</u>.   _____

2 I <u>jumped</u> into a puddle.   _____

3 Ren was <u>taking</u> driving lessons.   _____

What do I know?

1. I can choose synonyms for words.

2. I understand that words can have more than one synonym.

3. I can consider the differences between near-synonyms.

4. I can choose antonyms for words.

5. I understand that words can have more than one antonym, or no clear antonyms.

6. I can choose effective antonyms for some words.

1: What is formal and informal language?

Activity 1

Grammar guide

> The work you did is OK.

> The work you completed is acceptable.

- Language's register is the kind of tone it has or impression it makes.
- The everyday language people use in speech and casual writing is in an **informal register**.
- A **formal register** is likely to be used in official settings and documents, and when being polite is particularly important. For example, someone may use a formal register for a job application, a school report or a letter to someone they don't know.
- A register often relies on the vocabulary used.

Label each sentence as formal or informal.

1. They gathered sufficient evidence to conduct the trial. _____

2. School's kind of the same every day, I guess. _____

3. Thanks for offering your seat – but I'm OK standing up. _____

4. Ms Jain has become quite concerned about these difficulties. _____

5. I am writing to apologise for the misunderstanding. _____

Activity 2

| for sure | definitely | indubitably |

- Selecting formal language often means choosing between synonyms.
- Formal language does not just mean 'fancy' language. Its main aim is clarity, so 'indubitably' would rarely be the best of the synonyms above.

Draw lines to match each term on the left to its more formal synonym.

clever	retain
very	extremely
keep	consider
find out	in my opinion
think about	children
kids	intelligent
I think	discover

Activity 3

Write the meaning of each formal word.

1 subsequently _____

2 fabricate _____

3 amicable _____

2: Choosing formal or informal vocabulary

Activity 1

- A formal register relies greatly on the vocabulary chosen.
- Selecting formal language often means choosing between synonyms with different registers.

Rewrite the paragraph, changing each of the underlined terms to one of the formal alternatives below. Use each formal word only once.

tolerate   inform   problematic

litter   increasingly

Councillor, we need to <u>tell</u> you that the issue of the <u>rubbish</u> dropped on our streets is becoming <u>more and more</u> <u>tricky</u>. People will not <u>put up with</u> this for much longer.

<u>Councillor, we need to inform you</u>

_____

_____

_____

_____

_____

Activity 2

Grammar guide

From **whom** did you get a letter? | **Who** did you get a letter *from*?

- The relative pronoun '**whom**' is usually used in only formal language.
- It is used rather than '**who**' as the object in a sentence.
- In formal language, a **preposition** should never be placed at the end of a sentence. It comes before the object of the sentence instead.

Rewrite each sentence using vocabulary that is more formal.

1 Sorry for showing up late.

I apologise for _____

2 Who shall I hand over the present to?

_____

3 I think you can guess what the letter's about.

_____

4 Thanks for our chat, but I still don't get the problem.

_____

Activity 3

Complete the table of formal and informal vocabulary options.

Formal vocabulary	Informal vocabulary
	hi
to permit	
regarding	
	chatting
to improve	
	to look at

3: Formal and informal sentence stuctures

Activity 1

Grammar guide

We can go, **can't we**?

- **Question tags** can be added to sentences in informal language.
- They imply a conversation by speaking directly to the reader or listener.

Underline the question tag in each sentence.

1 Cara does know she helped, doesn't she?

2 You aren't going to be long, are you?

3 I have answered all the questions, haven't I?

Activity 2

Grammar guide

You **asked** that Jai **attend** the meeting.
He **instructed** that the room **be** cleaned.
I **wish** you **were** there when I needed you.

- The subjunctive is a formal way of stating something that hasn't happened, such as something **requested, commanded or wished**.
- In the third person, present-tense verbs other than 'be' take the **infinitive form**.
- The verb 'to be' becomes either 'be' or 'were'.
  - The form **'be'** is used when something may happen, for example when wishing or insisting that something will be the case in the future.
  - The form **'were'** is used when something is definitely not happening, for example when wishing that something happened in the past.

Tick the sentences that use subjunctive verb forms correctly.

- They requested that I be here on time. ☐
- I wish that it be sunny last weekend. ☐
- Mr Tiernan commands that his class were attentive. ☐
- It is vital that Chitra have the medicine. ☐
- If only it were not true. ☐
- I wish Ahab was home already. ☐
- Mei look up to the sky. ☐

Activity 3

Label each sentence as formal or informal. Underline the part of each sentence that shows its register.

1 The headteacher demands that Rod send a letter of thanks.

_____

2 He will do it, won't he?

_____

3 You really think so, don't you?

_____

4 If he were more grateful, he would.

_____

4: Using formal and informal structures

Activity 1

Grammar guide

> You **have** been to the bakery, **haven't** you?
> You **didn't** pick up the cake, **did** you?

- Question tags can be added to sentences in informal language.
- The **subject** of the tag matches, or is a pronoun for, the original sentence's **subject**.
- The verb in the tag is 'be', '**have**', 'should', 'could' or 'would', if any of these are in the original sentence. If they are not, the verb is always '**do**'.
- If the verb in the main sentence is <u>positive</u>, the verb in the question tag is <u>negative</u>. If the verb in the main sentence is <u>negative</u>, the verb in the question tag is <u>positive</u>.
- The verbs in the question tags are often in the form of contractions.

Add a question tag to each sentence.

1 It should work now, <u>shouldn't it?</u>

2 They take everything they can get, _____

3 Isaac hasn't eaten the last doughnut, _____

4 Gemma is coming over at eight o'clock, _____

Activity 2

Grammar guide

- The subjunctive form states something that hasn't happened.
- In the third person, present-tense verbs other than 'be' take the infinitive form.
- For the verb 'to be', the form 'be' is used when something may happen, and 'were' is used when it will not.

Rewrite each sentence using the subjunctive form.

1 Chris commanded loudly that Tom closes the window.

   Chris commanded loudly that Tom close the window.

2 Miriam's father insists that she practises her cello every night.

   _____

3 If only this was a more interesting subject.

   _____

4 Our teacher demands that the desks are tidy.

   _____

Activity 3

Rewrite the formal sentence in an informal register. Rewrite the informal sentence in a formal register.

It is necessary that we be cautious.

_____

It's important this goes OK, isn't it?

_____

5: Choosing a register

Activity 1

Grammar guide

- Some situations are best suited to a formal register.
- Other situations are best suited to an informal register.
- To choose a register, you could think about how familiar and comfortable you are with the person or people you're addressing, and well as how official the situation is.

1 Tick the contexts that would be best suited to a formal register.

- a written essay for school ⬜
- a note to a friend ⬜
- a letter applying for a summer job ⬜
- a social media post ⬜
- an official apology ⬜

2 Do you think the register of each paragraph is suitable for the given text type? Explain your ideas below each paragraph.

a A job application:

> Dear Ms Lewis,
> I am writing to you in application for the position of a sales assistant. I would be delighted to meet you, were a suitable role to be available.

_____

_____

b A message on social media:

> Hello, Kevin. It is excellent to see you online. I have hoped to speak with you further ever since we said our farewells at school today.

_____

_____

c A book review:

> I'm not sure I like this book. I think it's kind of a sad ending, isn't it? It was like the guy who wrote it didn't like his own characters. I mean, they weren't great people, were they, but they didn't deserve what they got.

_____

_____

Activity 2

> Circle the more suitable options to complete each paragraph.

1 RMS Titanic was a **boat /** (**passenger liner**) that **sank / went down** in 1912 after **smashing into / striking** an iceberg **on / during** her first **voyage / trip**. **About / Approximately** 1,500 of the 2,208 people on board died.

2 Hi Jared – I'm having a **celebration / party** on Friday. We haven't seen each other in a **really long / considerable** time, **I believe. / have we?** It'd be **superb / great** if you **were to / could** find time to **attend / come**.

Activity 3

Before completing each task, choose which register you will use. As you write, consider:

- the accuracy of your Standard English
- your vocabulary
- your sentence structures.

Include at least one subjunctive verb and one question tag.

1 Write the first two or three sentences of an article about a change that you feel should be made to your school rules or your tasks at home.

_____

_____

_____

_____

_____

2 Write the first two or three sentences of a diary entry about a conversation you have had with your friends.

_____

_____

_____

_____

_____

What do I know?

1 I can recognise and use Standard English.

2 I can recognise formal and informal language.

4 I understand that question tags are informal, and can identify them.

3 I can choose formal or informal synonyms.

5 I understand that the subjunctive form is formal, and can identify it.

6 I can use question tags in informal sentences.

8 I can identify suitable and unsuitable writing styles for given contexts.

7 I can use the subjunctive form in formal sentences.

1: How can hyphens help with clarity?

Activity 1

Punctuation guide

Ana re-covered her damaged books while she recovered from the accident.

- **Hyphens** can be used to prevent ambiguity, in a way similar to commas.
- They can also completely change the meaning of a word or phrase.

Draw lines to show the meaning of each word.

re-sign	sent again
resign	sign again
re-sent	quit
resent	dislike

Activity 2

Punctuation guide

We found this adder, but there are **more dangerous** snakes.
We found this adder, but there are **more-dangerous** snakes.

- Hyphens can also change and clarify the meaning of a noun phrase.
- In the first example above, the **adverb** and **adjective** suggest two ideas: there are several snakes other than the adder, and they are all dangerous.
- In the second example, the **compound adjective** expresses one idea: the other snakes present more danger than the adder.

Read the following pairs of sentences. Explain the difference between their meanings.

1

I saw a man eating fish.

I saw a man-eating fish.

In the first sentence, a man was seen eating some fish.

In the second, _____

2

Sofia looked at the state of the art gallery.

Sofia looked at the state-of-the-art gallery.

_____

_____

3

She had three year-old children.

She had three-year-old children.

_____

_____

Activity 3

Read the following pair of sentences. A comma is used in one and a hyphen is used in the other. Explain the difference between the images they create.

It was a large, feathered bird.

It was a large-feathered bird.

_____

_____

2: Using hyphens for clarity

Activity 1

> **Punctuation guide**
>
> Hyphens can be used to prevent ambiguity or change the meaning of a word or phrase.

> Change the meaning of each sentence by adding a hyphen.

1 I resent your message.   <u>I re-sent your message.</u>

2 I recovered the picture.   _____

3 He was a fast, growing boy.   _____

4 Look at the whale watching boats.   _____

Activity 2

> Write two sentences for each phrase, one with a hyphen between the first two words of the phrase and one without.

1 most complete answers

<u>Javier had the most complete answers: he'd answered</u>

<u>27 questions.</u>

<u>Wendy gave the most-complete answers as hers included</u>

<u>examples.</u>

2 more exciting events

_____

_____

_____

_____

3 bird eating spiders

_____

_____

_____

_____

4 first class trip

_____

_____

_____

_____

Activity 3

Write one sentence of your own that has its meaning changed by the addition or removal of a hyphen. Write it once with the hyphen and once without.

_____

_____

_____

3: How are colons, semicolons and dashes used?

Activity 1

Punctuation guide

> I enjoy sport. I enjoy art, too. I enjoy music most **because** I sing quite well. I love performing. It's great!
> I enjoy sport; I enjoy art, too. I enjoy music most: I sing quite well. I love performing – it's great!

- **Colons**, **semicolons** and **dashes** can be used to connect clauses.
- They can be used in place of **full stops** and **conjunctions**.

> Underline the clauses in each sentence. Circle the punctuation mark that connects them. Label it 'colon', 'semicolon' or 'dash'.

1 Gorillas eat mainly plants; they will also, however, eat insects.

_____

2 The green light flashed: it was safe to cross the street.

_____

3 This is my favourite place for lunch – the pizzas are fantastic!

_____

Activity 2

I enjoy sport; I enjoy art, too. I enjoy music most: I sing quite well. I love performing – it's great!

- A **semicolon** can connect two main clauses of equal importance.
- A **colon** can introduce an example, a reason or an explanation.
- A **dash** could be used instead of a semicolon or colon, but in only informal writing.

Tick the sentences that use colons, semicolons and dashes correctly.

- Mum's shop is always busy; I can help out at weekends. ☐
- We acknowledge your request – our decision will be made shortly. ☐
- Simone had looked everywhere; including under the bed. ☐
- I enjoy helping to make dinner: cooking is really fun. ☐
- Hurry up – the race's about to start! ☐
- Are you feeling cold: the window's open. ☐

Activity 3

Label each sentence to show whether the colon introduces an example, a reason or a consequence.

1. Fin looked around nervously: he'd heard a noise behind him. _____

2. The toy is mechanical: its legs are moved by cogs. _____

3. Vinnie wears great vintage clothes: his hat is from the 1950s. _____

4: Using colons, semicolons and dashes

Activity 1

- Colons, semicolons and dashes can be used to connect clauses.
- A colon can introduce an example, a reason or an explanation.
- A semicolon can connect two main clauses of equal importance.
- A dash could be used instead of a colon or semicolon, but only in informal writing.

Add a colon, a semicolon or a dash to each sentence. Use each only once.

1. Deb said you went home early —— are you OK?

2. We should choose a gift for Veta —— it's her party on Saturday.

3. Yves picked a handful of flowers —— he would arrange them when he got home.

Activity 2

Look at the following passage and then rewrite it below. Change some of the full stops and conjunctions to colons, semicolons and dashes. After the example, use each only once.

Emir shivered. He hadn't worn nearly enough layers. The clock just had struck ten so he'd been waiting at the station for three hours now. The night was dark and the wind was cold. His cousin should have been there to meet him. However, no one had arrived. Suddenly, the gate creaked. Someone was coming!

<u>Emir shivered: he hadn't worn nearly enough layers.</u>

Activity 3

Look at the following long sentence and then rewrite it below. Change some of its colons, semicolons and dashes to full stops and conjunctions. Make the new sentences clear and effective.

I've been waiting for my cousin: he was meant to be here hours ago; he hasn't arrived – I'm giving up hope: I'd appreciate a lift – I need to find Rose Cottage; it may be nearby.

5: What are quotations?

Activity 1

What does the character Randolph have for breakfast? Use evidence from the text in your answer.
This is what the text says: 'Randolph had a bowl of cereal.'
The text says that he 'had a bowl of cereal'.

- Questions about a piece of writing often ask for evidence from the text. The most direct way of giving this evidence is using a **quotation**.
- A quotation is a word or words taken directly from another piece of writing. They are punctuated a lot like direct speech, within **single inverted commas**.
- The words in a quotation must be written exactly as they were written in the original, including the capital letters and any **punctuation** that is inside the inverted commas.
- If there was no end punctuation included, the whole sentence's end punctuation goes outside the inverted commas.
- Quotations that are main clauses, including full sentences, should come after an **introduction main clause and a colon**.
- Quotations that are words or phrases should become part of a sentence.

Read the short paragraph and question below.

When Tobias Smeckleby arrived at Pinkhurst Academy, everybody thought he was the most mean-looking teacher they'd ever known. Even the other teachers thought this was true. He had a sharp, mean voice. He had a sharp, mean stare. He also had a sharp, mean response if they said even just 'good morning' to him.

What did people think about Tobias Smeckleby when he arrived at Pinkhurst Academy?

Now tick the answers that use a quotation correctly.

- People thought he was 'the most mean-looking teacher they'd ever known.'
- People thought he was a 'mean-looking teacher.'
- Everyone thought the same thing: 'he was the most mean-looking teacher they'd ever known.'
- Everybody thought 'he was really mean-looking.'
- People thought: 'He was the most mean-looking teacher they'd ever known'
- People thought he was 'mean-looking'.

Activity 2

Detention with Mr Smeckleby could be terrifying.

1 Include all of the text above as a quotation in a sentence.

_____

2 Include just the underlined word as a quotation in a sentence.

_____

Activity 3

Look again at the paragraph in Activity 1. Answer each question below in a full sentence that includes a correctly punctuated quotation. Use one full-sentence quotation that comes after an introduction clause and a colon, and one phrase that is placed inside its sentence.

1 What was the new teacher's name?

_____

2 What was the new teacher's voice like?

_____

6: What are ellipses?

Activity 1

Punctuation guide

> We spent the night **talking, watching movies and** eating pizza.
> We spent the night … eating pizza.

- An **ellipsis** is a punctuation mark that looks like three full stops.
- Ellipses (the plural of 'ellipsis') show that **some words** are left out.
- When words are replaced by an ellipsis, the remaining words should still work together as a sentence.

1 Look at each pair of sentences. Underline the words in the first sentence that have been left out in the second one.

a The benefits of zoos have been questioned and debated by experts.
The benefits of zoos have been … debated by experts.

b Once Owen starts talking about comics, he goes on and on and on and on and on and on.
Once Owen starts talking about comics, he goes on and on …

c Air travel contributes greatly to climate change, although it is sadly often the cheapest and easiest option for holiday-goers.
Air travel … is … the cheapest and easiest option for holiday-goers.

2 Look again at part (c) above. Why might someone criticise the way the ellipsis has been used?

_____

_____

_____

Activity 2

Tick the sentences in which an ellipsis has been used correctly.

1 The news revealed the truth about the crime, the criminal and the victims.

- The news revealed the truth about ... the victims. ☐
- The news ... the crime, the criminal and the victims. ☐
- The news revealed ... the truth about the ... victims. ☐
- The news revealed ... the crime ... and the victims. ☐

2 The rights of our people to both freedom and security remain vital.

- The rights of our people ... remain vital. ☐
- The ... both freedom and security remain ... ☐
- The rights of our people to ... security ... remain vital. ☐
- The rights of our people to ... freedom ... remain vital. ☐

Activity 3

Punctuation guide

The figure turned around, and I finally saw his face. It was ...

Chapter 2

... Santana! I had never even considered him as a suspect.

- Ellipses can also build tension across breaks in text.
- In these cases, they replace words that have been left out of the first sentence so they can be moved to the next sentence ...
- ... and words that have been left out of the second sentence because they have already been used in the first one.

How do you think an ellipsis might create tension?

_____

_____

7: Using ellipses

Activity 1

Punctuation guide

- An ellipsis is a punctuation mark made up of three dots, like three full stops.
- Ellipses show that some words have been left out.

Use an ellipsis to leave out the underlined word or words in each sentence.

1 Our <u>general</u> work on water quality improves global health.

<u>Our ... work on water quality improves global health.</u>

2 Farah succeeded<u>, with one final, mighty push,</u> in opening the rusty window.

_____

3 The text suggests it was cold: 'there were icicles <u>like pointed teeth forming</u> along the roof'.

_____

4 The government admitted <u>today</u> that nurses <u>all over the country</u> deserve better pay.

_____

Activity 2

Punctuation guide

> **When did the character Sumitra get up, and when did she get to work?**
>
> The text says: 'Sumitra woke up early, **went to the gym** and got to work by nine o'clock.'
>
> The text says: 'Sumitra woke up early … and got to work by nine o'clock.'

- Using quotations is a valuable part of discussing pieces of writing.
- An **ellipsis** can be useful when you need to use only part of a quotation.
- In the example above, **the detail about the character going to the gym** doesn't answer the **question**, so it can be left out.
- When words are replaced by an ellipsis, the remaining words should always still work together in their sentence.

Read the passage below. Answer each question with a sentence containing **one** quotation containing **only** the information that's needed.

As Ro walked past the rusty gates, she felt cold and, when they creaked, suddenly afraid. The leaves that had fallen onto the road were being blown away. It was beginning to get dark and she could barely see where she was going. To make the problem worse, it was getting foggy. She hoped she would soon reach the safety of the cottage, its warmth and its comfort.

1 How did Ro feel as she walked past the gates?

The text says 'she felt cold and … afraid.'

2 How do we know it was a windy day?

The text says _____

3 Why was it hard for Ro to see where she was going?

The text says _____

4 What did Ro appreciate about the cottage?

The text says _____

Activity 3

Punctuation guide

- Ellipses can help to make links across breaks in text for effect.
- In these cases, they replace words that have been left out of the first sentence so they can be moved to the next sentence …
- … and words that have been left out of the second sentence because they have already been used in the first one.

Imagine that you are writing a story with chapters. Write two or three sentences to end the first chapter and start the next one, using an ellipsis to break up a sentence to create tension.

For example:

I put the key in the lock and turned it. The door slowly creaked open …

Chapter 2

… and there it was: the lost treasure!

Your answer:

_____

_____

Chapter 2

_____

_____

8: Exploring lists

Activity 1

Punctuation guide

At all times, I had **my keys, my wallet, my phone and my headphones.** There were four things I had at all times: my keys, my wallet, my phone and my headphones.

- A list is a series of connected things.
- Most **items in a list** are separated by **commas**.
- The last two items are connected with '**and**', not separated by a comma.
- You can begin a list using **a main clause as an introduction** and then a **colon**.

1 Put these items into a list **within** a main clause.

photographs | music | videos | movies

I scrolled through my _____

_____

2 Put these items into a list that comes after an introduction clause and a colon.

football | basketball | cricket | rugby

_____

_____

Activity 2

Punctuation guide

> Moe wrapped the hat, which was for her brother; a game for her sister; this book, which was for her mother and a jumper for her father.

- If any items other than the last one already contain **commas**, the items are separated by **semicolons** rather than more commas.
- The last two items are still separated by 'and' rather than with another semicolon.

1 Tick the sentences that punctuate lists in the correct way.

- Mikhail looked out at his garden; the valley below it, where mist was beginning to settle; the trees and the river. ◯
- We took oat cookies, soft, gooey brownies and cupcakes. ◯
- Dad unpacked vegetables; pasta; ice-cream; which was already melting; and fruit. ◯
- Dillon's favourite holidays had been at the beach, where the gull ate Dad's chips; camping in the forest and visiting the theme park, even though he got dizzy. ◯
- Karlo was learning to do breaststroke; how to swim longer distances and how to hold his breath underwater. ◯

2 Put these items into a list sentence. You can choose whether to put them inside a main clause or to use an introduction clause with a colon.

noisy seagulls   the sunlight, which gleamed on the waves

the wide, sandy beach   an ice-cream van

_____

_____

Activity 3

Punctuation guide

> For my breakfast I had fruit, cornflakes, eggs, and toast **and** marmalade.

If either of the last two items in a list contains '**and**', there is a **comma** (or semicolon) before the 'and' used for the list.

Put these items into a list sentence, in this order. You can choose whether to put them inside a main clause or to use an introduction clause with a colon.

| sandwiches | burgers | fish and chips | salad |

_____

_____

_____

9: What are bullet points?

Activity 1

Punctuation guide

- Some lists, especially ones with complicated items, use bullet points.
- A bullet is a punctuation mark (•). It looks a little like a large full stop that's positioned higher up, next to a word.
- Each item in a bulleted list is on a new line, with a bullet before it.
- There is no 'and' between the final two points.
- A bulleted list could put an introduction sentence, clause or phrase on a line above the first item, possibly with other text before it.
- The bullet points in this punctuation guide do not use an introduction sentence.

Nana and I bought:

- milk from the dairy near our village,
- cheese that the farmer makes herself,
- eggs from a nearby farm,
- bread baked by one of our neighbours.

Look at the list above and then answer these questions.

1 How many points are in the list above? _____

2 Write down the introduction words.

_____

Do they make up a full sentence? _____

Before you start Activity 2, look at the punctuation in the list above.

Activity 2

Punctuation guide

- There are different ways to punctuate bullet points, but all of the items in one list should be written in the same way.
- Look at the two bulleted lists below, in this punctuation guide.

If the items in a bulleted list are full sentences, do the following things.

  o Write each bullet as a normal sentence, with a capital letter and a full stop.
  o Make sure the introduction is a full sentence too, ending with a full stop.

If the items are not written as full sentences, the introduction should end in a colon. This means it will not be a full sentence, but it could be a main clause. The items:

  o should not start with capital letters
  o could end with commas or no punctuation, but this must be the same for all items except the last one
  o could continue on from an introduction clause or phrase, as though they are completing its sentence
  o should have a full stop at the end of the final item.

1 Look at the bulleted lists below. The introduction words are all correct, but only one set of items is punctuated correctly. Circle all of the mistakes in the other two sets.

We ate:
- chicken,
- potatoes
- I had carrots.

We ate lots of things:
- chicken
- potatoes
- carrots.

We ate lots of things:
- My mum had chicken,
- Navya had potatoes,
- and I had carrots

2 Rewrite the two incorrect lists above, correcting the mistakes.

Activity 3

Punctuation guide

- Semicolons can be used instead of commas or no punctuation at the end of list items that are not full sentences. The last item still has a full stop.
- List items that are main clauses can be linked by semicolons, like normal sentences. They still come after an introduction that is a full sentence.
  - Like in this bulleted list, the first item starts with a capital letter;
  - items after that do not, because they continue the sentence;
  - the final sentence ends with a full stop.

Changing just one thing in each list below would make the punctuation correct. Rewrite the list items (not the introductions) and correct them.

When you practise, you should:
- warm up your instrument;
- play your scales
- rehearse the song.

Practice includes several steps.
- Warm up your instrument;
- Play your scales;
- rehearse the song.

10: Writing bulleted lists

Activity 1

Punctuation guide

- There are different ways to punctuate bullet points, but all of the items in one list should be written in the same way.
- If the items are not written as full sentences:
  - the introduction should end in a colon
  - the items could continue on from it, completing its sentence
  - the items should not start with capital letters
  - most items could end with commas, semicolons or no punctuation, although this must be the same throughout the list
  - the last item should end with a full stop.

Change this list sentence to a list of bullet points.

Doors along the street were coloured purple, grassy green and a deep blue colour, like the sea.

Doors along the street were coloured _____

_____

_____

_____

_____

Activity 2

Punctuation guide

- If the items in a bulleted list are full sentences, they can be punctuated in different ways.
- Each sentence could keep its capital letter and full stop, after an introduction that is a full sentence too.
- The sentences could be linked by semicolons.
  - The first item would start with a capital letter;
  - items after that would not, because they continue the sentence;
  - the final sentence would end with a full stop.
- Alternatively, if full sentences all start the same way (like 'This means', as shown below), you could use their start as an introduction and the rest of each sentence as a bullet point. This means:
  - each point could complete the introduction phrase
  - it becomes a clause in a longer sentence, even if it is a main clause
  - it is not punctuated as a full sentence on its own.

Change these sentences to a list of bullet points.

After accidentally destroying the birthday cake, I had several options. I could leave the party immediately, without telling anyone. I could dash out and buy a new cake, hoping no one would notice before I got back. I could find my friend and confess, and hope she'd forgive me.

After accidentally destroying the birthday cake,

Activity 3

Rewrite both your answer to Activity 1 and your answer to Activity 2, punctuating each bulleted list in an alternative way.

Answer to Activity 1:

1

Answer to Activity 2:

2

What do I know?

1 I understand how a hyphen can clarify or change the meaning of a word or phrase.

2 I can alter a word's or phrase's meaning by adding a hyphen.

3 I understand how colons, semicolons and dashes can connect clauses in different ways.

6 I understand that ellipses can show that words have been left out, and what effects this can have.

4 I can choose colons, semicolons or dashes to connect clauses in writing.

7 I can use ellipses to replace some words in quotations and to make links across breaks in text.

5 I can use a word or words taken directly from another piece of writing as a quotation.

8 I understand how semicolons can be used in lists.

9 I understand the different ways to punctuate bulleted lists.

10 I can write and correctly punctuate bullet points.

70

I: What features are found in non-fiction?

Look at the text below. This is an information text that would act as an advert for an activity centre.

Radcliffe Activity Centre Re-opens!

After over a year of renovations, your local activity centre is back up and running! While we've been away, we've spruced up our sports spaces and cleared the craft rooms so all of our activities can be done in style, with the most up-to-date equipment available for everyone.

A lot of our popular classes and workspaces will return, as well as the Saturday afternoon film club and Sunday afternoon kids' club. You'll see a lot of new activities on offer, too. Whether you're planning a marathon or a masterpiece, or you fancy ballet or basketball, we think we've got you covered!

Have a look at our class schedule below to see what we've got going on during our first weekend.

What's new?

We can now offer:
- three rooms dedicated to daytime classes;
- freely available art equipment, including easels and a potter's wheel;
- a large astroturf games pitch;
- a state-of-the-art gym and training space.

	Room 1	Room 2	Room 3	Games pitch	Gym
Saturday 12 pm	Film club	Sculpture	Ballet	Rugby	Rowing
Saturday 4 pm		Life drawing	Ballroom dancing	Basketball	Weight training
Sunday 12 pm	Kids' club	Pottery	Improvisation	Football	Aerobics
Sunday 4 pm		Portraits	Drama	Hockey	Speed training

Activity 1

Grammar guide

- Non-fiction texts include information texts, instructions, news reports and posters. They use different features to present information.
- Headings and subheadings can tell the reader quickly what writing is about.
- Bullet points can present different pieces of listed information clearly.
- Tables can present information that relates to two different things in a way that's easy to understand. They let a reader find the information they want quickly, by looking at the column and row headings.
- Columns can break up longer passages of text and make them easier to read.
- Text in columns is read from the top to the bottom of one column and then from the top to the bottom of the next one.

Add labels to the information text on page 71 to show which feature is which.

sub-heading   table   heading

bullet points   columns of text

Activity 2

1. Why do you think columns have been used? Think about how the text looks, as well as how it is read.

_____

_____

2. What effect does the sub-heading have?

_____

_____

In Room 1, there's film club during the afternoon on Saturday and kids' club during the afternoon on Sunday. In Room 2 on Saturday, there's sculpture at 12 pm and life drawing at 4 pm. In Room 2 on Sunday, there's pottery at 12 pm and portraits at 4 pm. In Room 3 on Saturday, there's ballet at 12 pm and ballroom dancing at 4 pm. In Room 3 on Sunday, there's improvisation at 12 pm and drama at 4 pm. On the games pitch on Saturday, there's rugby at 12 pm and basketball at 4 pm. On the games pitch on Sunday, there's football at 12 pm and hockey at 4 pm. In the gym on Saturday, there's rowing at 12 pm and weight training at 4 pm. In the gym on Sunday, there's aerobics at 12 pm and speed training at 4 pm.

3 **a** Compare the table to the paragraph above. How is the table helpful in presenting this information?

_____

_____

b Look at the table. When and where is the ballet lesson?

_____

c Look at the table. What happens in the gym at 4 pm on Sunday?

_____

Activity 3

1 Is there anything about the text's layout that you would change? Why is that?

_____

_____

2 What other information do you think this text could have included? How would you lay it out?

_____

_____

2: Using features of non-fiction texts

Activity 1

- Non-fiction texts use different features to present information.
- Headings and subheadings can tell the reader quickly what writing is about.
- Bullet points can present different pieces of listed information clearly.
- Tables can present information that relates to two different things in a way that's easy to understand.
- Columns can break up longer passages of text and make them easier to read.
- Text in columns is read from the top to the bottom of one column and then from the top to the bottom of the next one.

Look at the following summaries of information that could be in a non-fiction text about football. Next to each summary, note down the best way you could present the information on a page.

1	The scores in matches with different teams in the area, in different years	
2	An explanation of when the team formed and how they became more successful	
3	An indication that the next section of text will be about what matches the team has won	
4	Details of some important moments in the history of the team	
5	An indication that the whole text will be about a football team called the Radcliffe Rangers	

Activity 2

Imagine you are doing a science project about the minibeasts where you live. In these next two activities, you will write a report for the project, using the template in Activity 3. You will describe three minibeasts you know exist, give one fact about each one and present some data from an imagined investigation. (You will be given the data to use.)

1 What three minibeasts will you write about?

_____   _____   _____

2 Write a heading for the report. Try to summarise in one phrase what it will be about.

_____

_____

3 What do you already know about the three minibeasts you chose? Make notes for two or three short paragraphs of general background information.

You could include:

- where you live
- how common minibeasts generally are in your area
- where you see these minibeasts specifically
- how often you see them.

_____

_____

_____

_____

_____

_____

4 Write one fact about each minibeast you mentioned. These could be as simple as how big they are, what colour they are or whether or not they fly.

_____

_____

_____

_____

Activity 3

Write your report.

The information for your table is below. Simply complete 'A', 'B' and 'C' with the names of the minibeasts you chose, and add the numbers to the table in the template.

These data describe how many of each kind of minibeast we saw in different places. When we were near plant life, we saw 'A' 13 times, 'B' 6 times and 'C' 15 times. When we were near water, we saw 'A' 2 times, 'B' 19 times and 'C' 6 times. When we were near lots of buildings, we saw 'A' 4 times, 'B' 9 times and 'C' 14 times.

Heading:

_____

Background information in columns:

_____	_____
_____	_____
_____	_____
_____	_____
_____	_____

Facts in bullet points:

- _____

- _____

- _____

Data in table:

	A:	B:	C:
Near plant life			
Near water			
Near buildings			

What do I know?

1 I understand how headings, subheadings, bullet points, tables and columns can be used in non-fiction texts.

2 I can plan to organise different pieces of information in different ways.

3 I can use different features of non-fiction texts in writing.

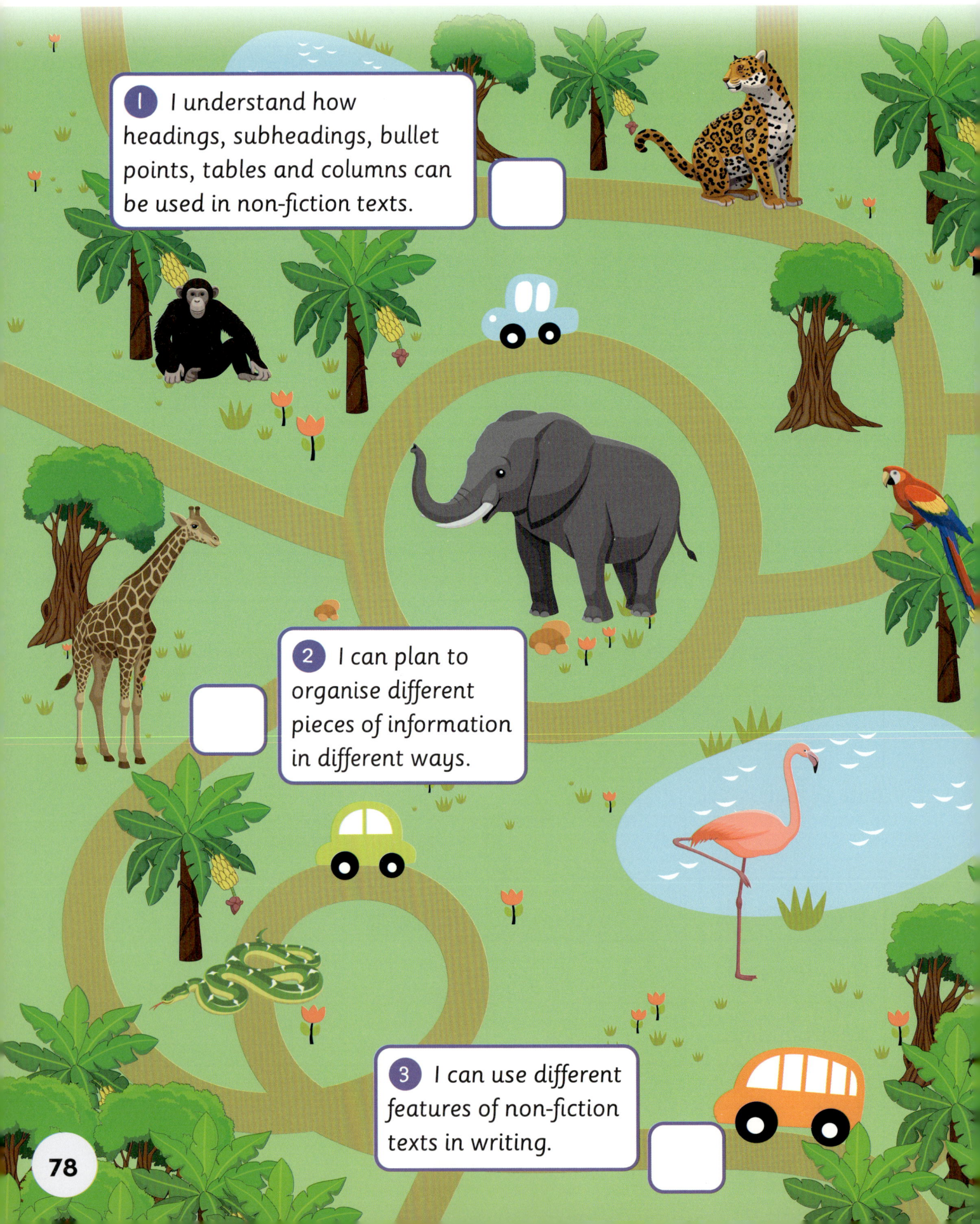

Here are some useful meanings. Key terms to understand are in orange.

Term	Meaning
Absolute adjective	An adjective that cannot have adverbials of degree such as 'more', 'very' or 'a bit' before it. For example: 'dead'; 'black'.
Active	The way in which the subject of a sentence is the thing or person performing the action named by the verb.
Adjectival phrase	A group of words that forms one piece of added information. Adjectival phrases include adverbials that add information to the head adjective. For example: 'the <u>completely dark</u> room'.
Adjective	A word that adds information to a noun. It describes what the thing named is like. For example: 'the <u>red</u> dress'.
Adverbial	A word (an adverb) or phrase that adds information to an adjective, verb or other adverb. Many adverbs end '–ly', but not all of them. For example: 'I ran <u>quickly</u>. I was tired <u>almost as soon as I started</u>.'
Agreement	The way in which all of the verb forms, nouns and other parts of a sentence match together in the right ways, such as in their tenses.
Alphabet	All the letters in order from A to Z. A list of words in alphabetical order starts with letters that come first in the alphabet. For example: 'apple, ball, cat …'.
Ambiguity	An unclearness of meaning. It relates to something that has more than one possible interpretation.
Antonym	Words or phrases that have opposite or very different meanings.
Apostrophe (')	A punctuation mark that can be used to show that letters have been missed out in a contraction or to show possession. For example: 'can't'; 'the horse's ears'.
Article	The words 'a', 'an', 'the' and 'some'. They are a type of determiner.

Term	Meaning
Attributive noun	Nouns that come before other nouns to affect and specify meaning, in a way similar to adjectives. However, they rarely describe what something is like but rather show what kind of thing it is, what it is for, where it is, what it is made from, or similar attributes. For example: 'car park'; 'geography teacher'.
Auxiliary verb	Verbs that are used to help create different forms of verbs. Forms of the auxiliary verb 'to be' are used in progressive tenses. Forms of the auxiliary verb 'to have' are used in perfect tenses. Within these verb forms, it is the auxiliary verb that changes to show tense and person.
Brackets ( )	Punctuation marks used in pairs that are placed around text to indicate that it is a parenthesis.
Bullet point (●)	A punctuation mark that appears before each item (or 'point') in some lists. Each point in a bulleted list begins on a new line and there is no 'and' between the final two points.
Capital letter	Large versions of letters. They could also be formed differently from the smaller letters they match. A capital letter is used at the start of a sentence or a name. For example: 'A'; 'B'; 'C'.
Clause	A group of words, including a subject and a verb, that means one thing but is not a full sentence.
Cohesion	The way in which sentences in a piece of writing are linked together to become effective as a whole. Writers can use cohesive devices to achieve this, such as fronted adverbials, repetition, rhyme and questions that are then answered (rhetorical questions).
Colon (:)	A punctuation mark used to mark an introduction. It could introduce a reason, example, explanation or items in a list.
Columns	A feature of non-fiction texts. They divide a page into vertical sections. The text in them is read from the top to the bottom of one column and then the top to the bottom of the next.
Comma (,)	A punctuation mark that separates items in a list and parts of a sentence that are not two clauses. It is often read as a short pause.

Term	Meaning
Command	A sentence that gives an instruction. Commands can be statements or exclamations, but they are never questions.
Comparative adjective	An adjective that compares the qualities of two or more nouns. Comparative adjectives are usually formed by the suffix '–er' or the addition of 'more' before the adjective. For example: 'This car is fast but that one is faster.' 'This story is exciting but that one is more exciting.'
Compound	A word that is formed when two shorter words are joined together, with or without a hyphen. For example: super + man = <u>superman</u>; more + dangerous = <u>more-dangerous</u>.
Conjunction	A word that links together sentences to form one longer sentence. In the new sentence, the original sentences become known as clauses.
Consonant	Any letter that is not a vowel.
Contraction	A word that has been shortened. Apostrophes in contractions show where letters have been missed out.
Coordinating conjunction	A conjunction that links two main clauses in a sentence.
Dash (–)	A punctuation mark that looks like a long hyphen. Dashes can be placed around text in informal writing to indicate it is a parenthesis, or used in place of a colon or semicolon in informal writing.
Definite determiner	A determiner that indicates something known and specific.
Definitive	Detail that is vital to meaning. For example: 'Please pass me only the pen <u>that is red</u>.'
Demonstrative	The words 'this', 'that', 'these' and 'those'. They can give basic information about whether something is singular ('this' and 'that') or plural ('these' and 'those'), and nearby ('this' and 'these') or far away ('that' and 'those'). They can be used as determiners or as pronouns.
Determiner	A word, which can be an article, that comes before a noun. Determiners can give basic information about whether something is singular or plural and definite or indefinite. For example: '<u>two</u> boxes'; '<u>all of the</u> things'.

Glossary

Term	Meaning
Dialogue	A conversation between two or more people, particularly one recorded in writing.
Direct speech	Writing that reports exactly what someone says. A sentence that includes direct speech shows the precise spoken words in speech marks (or 'inverted commas') and often an identifier.
Ellipsis (...)	A punctuation mark that shows that words have been left out, usually when only parts of a quotation are needed.
Exclamation	A sudden cry that shows surprise, excitement, shock or pain. It ends with an exclamation mark.
Exclamation mark (!)	A punctuation mark used at the end of a sentence, to show that the sentence is an exclamation.
Expanded noun phrase	A noun phrase that includes extra information about the thing named by the noun, for example using an adjective.
Fronted adverbial	An adverbial that comes at the start (front) of a sentence. It should be followed by a comma. For example: 'Suddenly, there was a crash.'
Full stop (.)	A punctuation mark used at the end of a sentence, to show that the sentence is a statement.
Future tense	A way of writing a verb to show that events or actions will happen in the future. It is formed by the modal auxiliary verb 'will' and an infinitive form without 'to'. For example: 'I will hurry.'
Future-perfect tense	A verb tense that shows that the action will have been completed before a particular time in the future. It is formed by the auxiliary verbs 'will have' and a past participle. For example: 'We will have watched the film before Friday.'
Future-progressive tense	A verb tense that shows an action that will continue over a period of time in the future. It is formed by the auxiliary verbs 'will be' and a present participle. For example: 'It will be raining all weekend.'
Heading	Words that appear as titles above pieces of writing. A heading tells the reader straight away what a piece of writing will be about.

Term	Meaning
Hyphen (-)	A punctuation mark, which in form is a short line. A hyphen joins words or parts of words together, to clarify meaning. For example: 'mother-in-law'; 're-cover'.
Identifier	A word that names the speaker of direct speech and includes a verb such as 'to say'. For example: "Hello," <u>said Gunther</u>.
Incidental	Detail (such as an incidental relative clause) that is not vital to meaning. For example: "I've found my pen, <u>which is red</u>."
Indefinite determiner	A determiner that indicates something general and non-specific.
Infinitive verb	The most basic form of a verb, preceded by 'to' (for example: 'to walk'; 'to be'). It expresses no tense and no person.
Inverted commas (" ") (' ')	Punctuation marks that show speech is being reported exactly. They are also known as speech marks. They can be double or single.
Irregular	Words that do not follow rules when they change. Verbs could have irregular tenses. Nouns could have irregular plurals.
Letter	A symbol used for writing. One group of letters makes up one word.
List	A series of connected things. For example: 'In the pond, there are <u>fish, frogs, toads and newts</u>.'
Main clause	A clause that gives the main point in a sentence. There can be more than one main clause in a sentence if they are equally important. If there are two main clauses joined by a conjunction in a sentence, swapping the order of two main clauses does not affect the meaning of the sentence.
Meaning	The thing or idea that a word, expression or sign represents.
Modal verb	A type of auxiliary verb that suggests degrees of possibility, ability or obligation. For example: 'I <u>must</u> go.' 'I <u>should</u> go.' 'I <u>may</u> go.'
Noun	A word that names a person, thing, event or idea.

Term	Meaning
Noun phrase	A group of words that all link to the thing named by the noun. A noun phrase could be as short as two words: a determiner and the noun.
Object	A noun, noun phrase or pronoun that is not the focus of a sentence. It comes after the verb. Usually, the object of a sentence is not doing the action named in the sentence, but it is involved in the action.
Paragraph	A clear section of a piece of writing, usually on the same topic. A new paragraph starts on a new line.
Parenthesis	A word, phrase or clause that has been added into a sentence as an explanation, aside or afterthought, but is not vital to meaning or the grammar of a sentence. It is marked by brackets, commas or dashes around it. For example: 'The wolf – a huge, slavering beast – prowled around the field.'
Passive	The way in which the person or thing performing an action is named as the object of the sentence. The passive voice can be used to emphasise the action rather than the person doing the action. Passive verbs are formed with the verb 'to be' and a past participle. For example: 'The ball is passed to Finbar.'
Past participle	A verb form used to form perfect tenses. A verb's past participle is usually the same as its past tense.
Past tense	A way of writing a verb to show that events or actions happened in the past.
Perfect tenses	Ways of writing a verb to show that an action is perfectly complete. They are formed with the auxiliary verb 'have', which is the verb that changes to show tense and person, and a past participle.
Person	The way in which a verb changes to show who or what does the action. Each person can be singular or plural. First person relates to oneself (for example: 'I'; 'we'). Second person relates to the direct recipient of a sentence (for example: 'you'). Third person relates to another person or thing named in the sentence (for example: 'she'; 'the cats').

Term	Meaning
Personal pronoun	Pronouns that represent grammatical persons. These include subject personal pronouns (for example: 'you'; 'they') and object personal pronouns (for example: 'me'; 'them').
Phrase	A group of words that means one thing but is not a full sentence. It could be as short as two words.
Plural	The way in which a noun or pronoun names more than one of a thing or a verb shows that more than one person or thing is doing the action.
Possession	Something that belongs to someone or something else. This could mean it is owned by them or is related to them in a different way.
Possessive noun	A noun that shows possession. The noun for the owner takes the possessive form. For singular nouns and plurals that do not end '–s', this is made up of the noun, an apostrophe and 's'. For plural nouns that end '–s', it is made up of the noun and an apostrophe.
Possessive pronoun	A word that stands in for a possessive noun. Possessive pronouns can be determiners (for example: 'my'; 'your') or they can be used independently, to mean the possessive noun and the thing that is owned (for example: 'mine'; 'yours').
Prefix	A group of letters added at the start of a word to change its meaning. For example: <u>un</u>happy; <u>re</u>play.
Preposition	A word that makes links between parts of a sentence. It usually comes at the beginning of a prepositional phrase (for example: 'along the street'; 'around the bend'; 'with a big smile'; 'after lunch'). A prepositional phrase can be part of a noun phrase (for example: 'I live in <u>the house along the street</u>') or be adverbials (for example: 'I live <u>along the street</u>').
Present participle	A verb form ending '–ing'. Present participles are used to form progressive tenses.
Present tense	A way of writing a verb to show that events or actions happen now or happen regularly.

Term	Meaning
Progressive tenses	Ways of writing a verb to show that an action continues over a period of time. They are formed with the auxiliary verb 'is', which is the verb that changes to show tense and person, and a present participle.
Pronoun	A word that stands in for a noun or noun phrase. The words 'I', 'you' singular, 'he', 'she', 'it', 'we', 'you' plural and 'they' are all pronouns.
Punctuation	The marks made in writing that are not letters. Punctuation makes writing easier to understand.
Quantitative determiner	Words that give information about quantity. For example: 'all'; 'some'; 'every'; 'three'.
Question	A sentence that is used to ask for information. It ends with a question mark.
Question mark (?)	A punctuation mark used at the end of a sentence, in place of a full stop, to show that a sentence is a question.
Question tag	Words that can be added at the end of a statement in informal writing, to turn it into a question. For example: 'It's hot, <u>isn't it?</u>' 'They speak quickly, <u>don't they?</u>'
Quotation	A word or words taken directly from another piece of writing. Similar to direct speech, quotations are written inside single inverted commas and often with an identifier.
Register	The level of how formal or informal a piece of writing or speech is. The everyday language people use in speech and casual writing is in an informal register. A formal register is likely to be used in official settings and documents, and when being polite is particularly important.
Relative clause	A type of subordinate clause that is introduced by a relative pronoun. The clause adds extra detail, so acts like an adjective. For example: 'Flora, <u>who was an explorer</u>, set off for the jungle.'
Relative pronoun	A word that opens a relative clause by referring back to the noun or noun phrase that precedes it. The relative pronouns are 'who', 'whom', 'whose', 'which', 'that', 'where' and 'when'.
Root word	A simple word that can be altered by different prefixes or suffixes to form a word family. For example: 'farm' in 'farming'; 'please' in 'pleasant'.

Term	Meaning
Semicolon (;)	A punctuation mark used to separate two main clauses in a sentence if they are of equal importance. Semicolons can also be used to separate items in a list, if any of the items already contain punctuation (such as commas).
Sentence	A group of words that means one whole thing. It gives a whole idea.
Singular	The way in which a noun or pronoun names only one thing, or a verb shows that one person or thing is doing the action.
Speech marks (" ") (' ')	Punctuation marks that show speech is being reported exactly. They are also known as inverted commas. They can be double or single.
Standard English	English that is grammatically correct.
Statement	A sentence that ends with a full stop rather than a question mark or an exclamation mark. A statement gives a piece of information.
Sub-heading	Titles that are smaller than headings. They appear before shorter sections within a piece of writing. Sub-headings can help guide a reader through a piece of writing.
Subject	The noun, noun phrase or pronoun that is the focus of a sentence. It is named first, before the verb. Usually, the subject of a sentence is the person or thing doing the action named by the verb.
Subjunctive	A formal way of forming a verb to name an action that hasn't happened, such as something requested, commanded or wished.
Subordinate clause	A clause that gives extra information that is not the key point in a sentence. There cannot be a subordinate clause in a sentence without a main clause. If a main clause and a subordinate clause are joined by a conjunction in a sentence, swapping their positions affects the meaning or makes no sense.
Subordinating conjunction	A conjunction that links a main clause to a subordinate clause in a sentence.
Suffix	A letter or group of letters added at the end of a word to change its meaning. For example: farming; farmer.

Term	Meaning
Superlative adjective	An adjective that compares the qualities of three or more nouns. Superlative adjectives show that the quality being described is the most extreme. They are usually formed by the suffix '–est' or the addition of 'the most' before the adjective. For example: 'Those cars are fast but that one is the fastest.' 'All the stories are quite exciting but that one is the most exciting.'
Synonym	Words or phrases that have the same or very similar meanings.
Table	Features of non-fiction texts that present information relating to two different things in a grid that is easy to understand. They let a reader find the information they want quickly, by looking at the column and row headings.
Tense	The way in which a verb shows when the action happens.
Verb	A word that names an action. Every sentence must contain at least one verb.
Vowel	The letters 'a', 'e', 'i', 'o' and 'u'.
Word	A group of letters that make up one unit of meaning. In writing, a word has a space on each side of it. In slow speech, a word has a short silence on each side of it.
Word family	A group of words with the same root word and related spellings. For example: 'farm', 'farmer', 'farming' and 'farmed'; 'please', 'displeasing', 'pleasant' and 'pleasantries'.

Answer key

Effective noun phrases

1: Exploring adjectives

Activity 1

1a. youngest; different

1b. much bigger

2a–b. [Children's answers will vary, but each must be an appropriate adjective or adjectival phrase.]

Activity 2

1. I read a better book last week. It had a more surprising twist at the end.

2. That's the funniest poem. It has the most amusing illustrations.

Activity 3

[Children's answers will be annotations on Activity 1, question 1.]

1a. superlative

1b. comparative

2: Exploring prepositions

Activity 1

1. The shed at the end of the garden [underlined once]; at the end of the garden [underlined twice]

2. The moon's reflection on the lake [underlined once]; on the lake [underlined twice]

3. The grey clouds above us [underlined once]; above us [underlined twice]

Activity 2

1a. on [underlined]; The stain on the carpet wouldn't come out. [ticked]

1b. over [underlined]

1c. through [underlined]; Our route through the city was blocked. [ticked]

1d. during [underlined]; The show during half time was amazing.

1e. at [underlined]

2a. I ran quickly through the tunnel. ['the tunnel' underlined]

2b–c. [Children's answers will vary, but each must add an appropriate prepositional phrase.]

Activity 3

[Children's answers will vary, but each must use the phrase as part of a noun phrase.]

3: Exploring relative clauses

Activity 1

1. when she could return home [underlined]; when [also circled]; time

2. that didn't make him sneeze [underlined]; that [also circled]; thing

3. to whom I wrote last week [underlined]; whom [also circled]; person

4. where we have to catch a bus [underlined]; where [also circled]; place

Activity 2

1a. who

1b. whose

1c. whom

2a–b. [Children's answers will vary, but each must be a definitive relative clause beginning: 2a. 'when'; 2b. 'where'.]

Activity 3

1. that; which

2. the cup that I was washing

4: Combining information in noun phrases

Activity 1

1. those warm hats in the shop that we found

2–3. [Children's answers will vary, but each must expand each noun phrase appropriately using one or more of the given options.]

Activity 2

1. That's the old lady with purple hair who smiles kindly.
2. I went back to the beautiful forest on the hill where we once had a picnic.
3. I saw an enormous bird with orange spots that was singing.
4. Philly is that young boy in the armchair who is waving.
5. That was the glorious day during the summer when we met.

Activity 3

1. She had a cat. The cat was fluffy. The cat had grey ears. The cat purred loudly.
2. We're going to the cinema. The cinema is new. The cinema is in town. There are sofas in the cinema.
3. He looked for the stranger. The stranger was kind. The stranger was on the train. The stranger had helped him.

[Children's wordings may vary slightly, but must give the correct information in four discrete sentences per question.]

Creating cohesion

1: Revising adverbials

Activity 1

Consequently: The next point is a result of the one before it.

In contrast: The next point contradicts the one before it.
In summary: The next point summarises all of the points before it. [Children's wordings may vary, but the senses of the adverbials must be described correctly.]

Activity 2

[Children's answers will vary, but each (after the first) must signal the following point's relationship to the previous one(s). For example: Currently; For example; However; On the other hand; In summary.]

Activity 3

[Children's answers will vary, but each must be a collection of alternative adverbials that could assist with structuring and/or relating ideas.]

2: What are cohesive devices?

Activity 1

1. The sentences ask and answer a question. They also repeat 'p' in 'promised' and 'presentation'.

2–3. [Children's answers must identify: 2. repetition; 3. questions and rhymes]

Activity 2

1. [Children's answers will vary, but each must be an engaging question and answer about the rainforest.]
2. [Children's answers will vary, but each must repeat a sound to create an engaging motto.]
3. [Children's answers will vary, but each must repeat words to create persuasive instructions.]

4. [Children's answers will vary, but each must use at least one rhyme to create an engaging advertising slogan about school clothes.]

Activity 3

[Children's answers will vary, but each must be a short paragraph that includes at least two of these devices: a question and answer / repetition of a word, phrase or sound / rhyming words.]

The passive voice

1: What is the passive voice?

Activity 1

1. She [circled]; magazine [underlined]
2. Georgie [circled]; apples [underlined]
3. Someone [circled]; pencils [underlined]
4. Kim and his mum [circled]; fruit and vegetables [underlined]

Activity 2

1. That play [circled]; all of us [underlined]; passive
2. Jayne and Li [circled]; modern art [underlined]; passive
3. You [circled]; active
4. Franco's letter [circled]; passive
5. Brad [circled]; old records [underlined]; active

Activity 3

The cake was eaten by Tina. – simple past, passive voice
We were running home. – past progressive, active voice
The ball has been kicked by Marco. – present perfect, passive voice
I was cold. – simple past, active voice

2: Using the passive voice

Activity 1

1. Ma is often helped by Asha.
2. The chest of drawers has been painted by us.
3. Fish are being caught by that heron.

Activity 2

[Children's answers will vary, but one option in each pair must be selected. In those sentences, children may or may not select the information in brackets.

Activity 3

1. The house was searched by me.
2. The house had been searched by me.
3. The house is being searched by me.

Synonyms and antonyms

1: What are synonyms?

Activity 1

come – arrive
sprint – run
show – display
false – fake
get – buy
grip – hold

Activity 2

1. The goalkeeper made a huge mistake.
2. Geraint used up all his money by renting movies.
3. That's his fresh bike.
4. Did you smash your brother's model?
5. Leah asked me for support at school.

Activity 3

[Children's answers will vary, but should acknowledge that there are differences in the meaning of the pairs, and are likely to identify that 'new' and 'fresh' are the most different in the context.]

2: Choosing synonyms carefully

Activity 1

1. owns [ticked]
2. arrangements [ticked]
3. performance [ticked]
4. strange [ticked]

Activity 2

1. One means they were just fast and the other means they were doing things more quickly than usual because they didn't have much time.
2. 'Hate' is more extreme than 'dislike'.
3. 'Wonder' implies being unsure and imaginative, and 'consider' suggests thinking carefully about something.
4. Unlike 'think', 'believe' suggests faith and a strong feeling about truth.

[Children's answers will vary, but each must show appreciation of the differences described here.]

Activity 3

[Children's answers will vary, but each must rewrite the sentences using appropriate synonyms. For example: On Thursday, Jakub travelled into town to buy a gift for his sister. He searched for ages for something she'd want. Finally, he discovered something perfect.]

3: What are antonyms?

Activity 1

love – hate
beautiful – ugly
friendly – unfriendly
wide – narrow
arrive – leave
good – bad

Activity 2

1. Sota was usually unhelpful around the house.
2. It always rains on her birthday.
3. That's the worst idea I've heard in ages!
4. It was impossible that they'd see him again.
5. I'm so disappointed you could get here!

Activity 3

[Children's answers will vary, but should acknowledge that the pairs are not always exact opposites, and are likely to identify that 'pleased' / 'disappointed' and/or 'certain' / 'impossible' seem least direct.]

4: Choosing effective antonyms

Activity 1

1a. bad; 1b. terrible
2a. cool; 2b. cold
3a. sad; 3b. devastated
4a. clear; 4b. obvious

Activity 2

1–3. [Children's answers will vary, but each must be three appropriate antonyms for: 1. 'interesting'; 2. 'frightened'; 3. 'soft', and rewrite each sentence using one of them.]

Activity 3
1–3. [Children's answers will vary, but each must create significantly different meanings for the sentences.]

Formal and informal registers

1: What is formal and informal language?

Activity 1
1. formal; 2. informal; 3. informal; 4. formal; 5. formal

Activity 2
clever – intelligent
very – extremely
keep – retain
find out – discover
think about – consider
kids – children
I think – in my opinion

Activity 3
1. e.g. as a result / afterwards
2. e.g. make up / invent / create
3. e.g. friendly
[Children's wordings may vary, but their comprehension of each term should be accurate.]

2: Choosing formal or informal vocabulary

Activity 1
Councillor, we need to inform you that the issue of the litter dropped on our streets is getting increasingly problematic. People will not tolerate this for much longer.

Activity 2
1–4. [Children's answers will vary, but must rephrase each sentence to use more-formal vocabulary.]

Activity 3
e.g. hello
e.g. to let
e.g. to do with
e.g. having a conversation
e.g. to get better / make better
e.g. to regard
[Children's wordings may vary, but their comprehension of each term must be accurate.]

3: Formal and informal sentence structures

Activity 1
1. doesn't she? [underlined]
2. are you? [underlined]
3. haven't I? [underlined]

Activity 2
They requested that I be here on time. [ticked]
It is vital that Chitra have the medicine. [ticked]
If only it were not true. [ticked]

Activity 3
1. send [underlined]; formal
2. won't he? [underlined]; informal
3. don't you? [underlined]; informal
4. were [underlined]; formal

4: Using formal and informal structures

Activity 1
1. shouldn't it?
2. don't they?
3. has he?
4. isn't she?

Activity 2
1. Chris commanded loudly that Tom close the window.
2. Miriam's father insists that she practise her cello every night.

3. If only this were a more interesting subject.
4. Our teacher demands that the desks be tidy.

Activity 3

e.g. We'd better be careful, hadn't we? It is important that this go well. [Children's wordings may vary, but their comprehension of each sentence must be accurate and their registers must be consistent.]

5: Choosing a register

Activity 1

1. a written essay for school [ticked]; a letter applying for a summer job [ticked]; an official apology [ticked]

2a–c. [Children's wordings will vary, but each answer must recognise that this is: (a) a formal register and is appropriate for the job application; (b) a formal register and is not appropriate for the message to a friend; (c) an informal register and is not appropriate for the book review.]

Activity 2

1. passenger liner; sank; striking; during; voyage; Approximately [each circled]
2. party; really long; have we?; great; could; come [each circled]

Activity 3

1–2. [Children's answers will vary, but each must be two or three sentences in Standard English and: 1. a formal register, including at least one subjunctive verb; 2. an informal register, including at least one question tag.]

Punctuation

1: How can hyphens help with clarity?

Activity 1

re-sign – sign again; resign – quit
re-sent – sent again; resent – dislike

Activity 2

[Children's wordings will differ, but comprehension of each sentence must be correct. For example:]
1. In the first sentence, a man was seen eating some fish. In the second, a fish that eats humans was seen.
2. In the first sentence, Sofia was looking at the condition of the art gallery. In the second, she was looking at a new, modern art gallery.
3. In the first sentence, she had three children who were all one year old. In the second, we are told that her children were three years old but not how many children there were.

Activity 3

[Children's wordings will differ, but comprehension of each sentence must be correct.
For example: In the first sentence, we are told that the bird was large and that it had feathers. In the second, we are told that the bird's feathers were large.]

2: Using hyphens for clarity

Activity 1

1. I re-sent your message
2. I re-covered the picture.

3. He was a fast-growing boy.
4. Look at the whale-watching boats.

Activity 2

1. Javier had the most complete answers: he'd answered 27 questions.
   Wendy gave the most-complete answers as hers included examples.
2. [Children's responses will vary, but each should be two sentences, one of which suggests that some events could be more exciting than others and one of which suggests that there is more than one other exciting event.]
3. [Children's responses will vary, but each should be two sentences, one of which mentions a bird that eats spiders and one of which mentions spiders that eat birds.]
4. [Children's responses will vary, but each should be two sentences, one of which mentions the first trip a class takes and one of which mentions a high-quality trip.]

Activity 3

[Children's answers will vary, but each must be two sentences that rely on a hyphen, and lack of a hyphen, for meaning.]

3: How are colons, semicolons and dashes used?

Activity 1

1. Gorillas eat mainly plants [underlined]; [semicolon circled] they will also, however, eat insects [underlined]; semicolon

2. The green light flashed [underlined]; [colon circled]; it was safe to cross the street [underlined]; colon
3. This is my favourite place for lunch [underlined]; [dash circled]; the pizzas are fantastic [underlined]; dash

Activity 2

Mum's shop is always busy; I can help out at weekends. [ticked]
I enjoy helping to make dinner: cooking is really fun. [ticked]
Hurry up – the race's about to start! [ticked]

Activity 3

1. reason
2. explanation
3. example

4: Using colons, semicolons and dashes

Activity 1

1. – [dash]
2. : [colon]
3. ; [semicolon]

Activity 2

[Children's answers will vary, but each must connect some sentences with colons, semicolons or dashes to form a clear, effective paragraph.]

Activity 3

[Children's answers will vary, but each must replace some colons, semicolons or dashes with end punctuation or conjunctions to form a clear, effective paragraph.]

5: What are quotations?

Activity 1
People thought he was 'the most mean-looking teacher they'd ever known.' [ticked]
Everybody thought the same thing: 'he was the most mean-looking teacher they'd ever known.' [ticked]
People thought he was 'mean-looking'. [ticked]

Activity 2
1. This is what the text says: 'Detention with Mr Smeckleby could be terrifying.' [Children's wording of the introduction clause will vary, but it should be a main clause and the punctuation and structure of the sentence must be correct.]
2. The text says that detention with Mr Smeckleby could be 'terrifying'. [Children's wording will vary, but the punctuation of the sentence must be correct.]

Activity 3
1. The (text says the) new teacher's name was 'Tobias Smeckleby'.
2. This is what the text says: 'He had a sharp, mean voice.'
[Children's wording outside of the quotations will vary, but the punctuation of the sentences must be correct.]

6: What are ellipses?

Activity 1
1a. questioned and [underlined]
1b. and on and on and on and on [underlined]
1c. contributes greatly to climate change, although it; sadly often [each underlined]

2. [Children's answers will vary, but must acknowledge that the main point has been left out so the sentence's meaning has changed.]

Activity 2
1. The news revealed the truth about … the victims. [ticked]
   The news revealed … the crime … and the victims. [ticked]
2. The rights of our people … remain vital. [ticked]
   The rights of our people to … security … remain vital. [ticked]
   The rights of our people to … freedom … remain vital. [ticked]

Activity 3
[Children's answers will vary, but should acknowledge that the ellipses suggest the text pauses in the middle of an action, making the reader want to discover its conclusion.]

7: Using ellipses

Activity 1
1. Our … work on water quality improves global health.
2. Farah succeeded … in opening the rusty window.
3. The text suggests it was cold: 'there were icicles … along the roof'.
4. The government admitted … that nurses … deserve better pay.

Activity 2
1. The text says 'she felt cold and … afraid.'
2. The text says 'leaves … were being blown away.'
3. The text says it was 'beginning to get dark and … it was getting foggy.'

4. The text says she appreciated its 'safety … warmth and … comfort.' [Children's answers may vary slightly but must give only relevant information in one precise quotation, and use ellipses correctly within it.]

Activity 3

[Children's answers will vary, but must split a sentence effectively over the text break.]

8: Exploring lists

Activity 1

1. I scrolled through my photographs, music, videos and movies.

2. e.g. My school offers these sports: football, basketball, cricket and rugby. [Children may vary the introduction clause, although this must remain a main clause and be followed by a colon.]

[For both 1. and 2. children may vary the order of the items in the list, but must punctuate them correctly.]

Activity 2

1. Mikhail looked out at his garden; the valley below it, where mist was beginning to settle; the trees and the river. [ticked]
Dillon's favourite holidays had been at the beach, where the gull ate Dad's chips; camping in the forest and visiting the theme park, even though he got dizzy. [ticked]

2. [Children's answers will vary, but must punctuate the list correctly using semicolons. For example: I could see noisy seagulls; the wide, sandy beach; an ice-cream van and the sunlight, which gleamed on the waves.]

Activity 3

[Children's answers will vary, but each must punctuate the list correctly with a comma before the final 'and'. For example: The menu included sandwiches, burgers, fish and chips, and salad.]

9: What are bullet points?

Activity 1

1. Four / 4
2. Nana and I bought
   No.

Activity 2

1. Left box: the comma after the word 'chicken' or the lack of a comma after the word 'potatoes'; the words 'I had' [each circled]
Right box: both commas; the word 'and'; the lack of punctuation after the end of the word 'carrots' [each circled]
The central box should not be marked.

2a. We ate:
   - chicken,
   - potatoes,
   - carrots.

[Children could choose to use no punctuation instead of the two commas.]

2b. We ate lots of things.
   - My mum had chicken.
   - Navya had potatoes.
   - I had carrots.

Activity 3

1.
   - warm up your instrument;
   - play your scales;
   - rehearse the song.

2.
- Warm up your instrument;
  - play your scales;
  - rehearse the song.

[Children could choose to remove the semicolon after 'instrument' rather than to add one after 'scales'.]

10: Writing bulleted lists

Activity 1
[Children's answers will vary, but the list should use correctly punctuated bullet points in one consistent style.]

Activity 2
[Children's answers will vary, but the list should use correctly punctuated bullet points in one consistent style.]

Activity 3
[Children's answers will vary, but each of the two lists should use correctly punctuated bullet points in one consistent style per list, differently from the way they were punctuated in Activities 1 and 2.]

Non-fiction features

1: What features are found in non-fiction?

Activity 1
[Labels should be added to the correct features on the information text.]

Activity 2
[Children's wordings for Questions 1–3a. will vary, but each should appreciate the purpose of each feature.]
1. The columns break up the text on the page so it looks more interesting, and to make it easier to read.

2. The sub-heading tells the reader what the next section of text will be about.
3a. The table presents the information more clearly than the paragraph. This is because it is easier to find the facts you need by reading the column and row headings.
3b. Saturday 12 pm in Room 3
3c. Speed training

Activity 3
1–2. [Children's answers will vary but should be justified.]

2: Using features of non-fiction texts

Activity 1
1. in a table
2. in paragraphs / columns
3. as a sub-heading
4. in bullet points
5. in the heading

Activity 2
1–4. [Children's answers will vary: they will be notes about content to use in a non-fiction text.]

Activity 3
[Children should fit their planned content into the template appropriately. The table should be populated as follows, using children's chosen minibeasts as column headings.]

	A	B	C
Near plant life	13	6	15
Near water	2	19	6
Near buildings	4	9	14